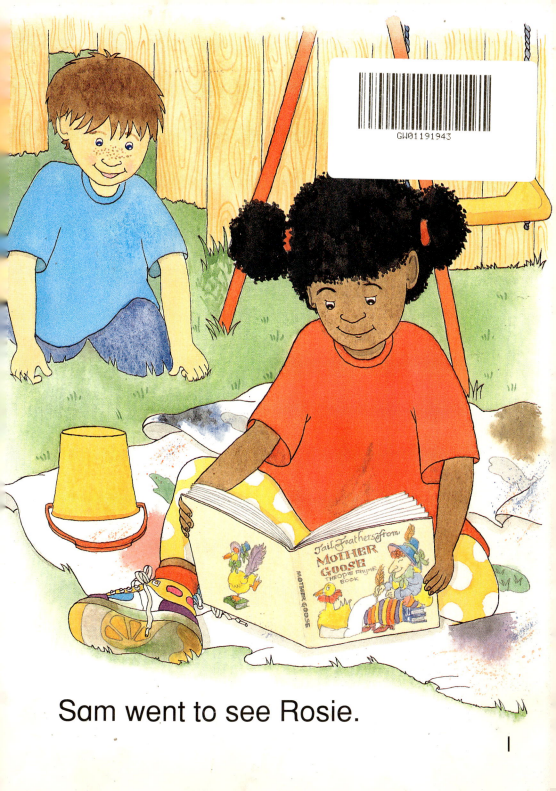

Sam went to see Rosie.

They played ghosts.

3

Rosie got a table.

Sam got some boxes.

Rosie got some buckets.

They made a train.

They made it bigger and

bigger and **bigger.**

Rosie said,
'Look, Grandad! It's a train.'

Grandad got on the train.

13

Crash!

Grandad said, 'It's a ghost train!'